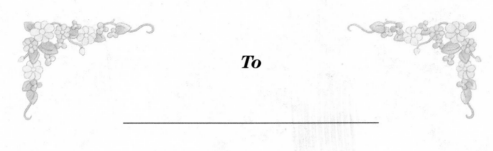

To

_____

From

_____

*Date*_____

Precious Moments of
Celebration

The Helen Steiner Rice Foundation

Whatever the celebration, whatever the day, whatever the event, whatever the occasion, Helen Steiner Rice possessed the ability to express the appropriate feeling for that particular moment in time.

A happening became happier, a sentiment more sentimental, a memory more memorable because of her deep sensitivity to put into understandable language the emotion being experienced. Her positive attitude, her concern for others, and her love of God are identifiable threads woven into her life, her works . . . and even her death.

Prior to her passing, she established the HELEN STEINER RICE FOUNDATION, a nonprofit corporation whose purpose is to award grants to worthy charitable programs and aid the elderly, the needy, and the poor. In her lifetime, these were the individuals about whom Mrs. Rice was greatly concerned.

Royalties from the sale of this book will add to the financial capabilities of the HELEN STEINER RICE FOUNDATION. Each year this foundation presents grants to various qualified, worthwhile, and charitable programs. Because of her foresight, her caring, and her deep convictions, Helen Steiner Rice continues to touch a countless number of lives. Thank you for your assistance in helping to keep Helen's dream alive.

Virginia J. Ruehlmann, Administrator
The Helen Steiner Rice Foundation
Suite 2100, Atrium Two
221 East Fourth Street
Cincinnati, Ohio 45202

Celebration

Verses by Helen Steiner Rice

Compiled by Virginia J. Ruehlmann

Illustrations by Samuel J. Butcher

Fleming H. Revell

A Division of Baker Book House
Grand Rapids, Michigan 49516

The endsheets,
enhanced with real flower petals,
ferns, and other botanicals,
are from
"The Petals Everlasting Collection"
manufactured by Permalin Products.

Text copyright 1993 by Helen Steiner Rice Foundation
Art copyright 1993 by PRECIOUS MOMENTS, Inc.

Published by Fleming H. Revell,
a division of Baker Book House
P.O. Box 6287, Grand Rapids, Michigan 49516-6287

Library of Congress Cataloging-in-Publication Data

Rice, Helen Steiner.
    Precious moments of celebration / verses by Helen Steiner Rice ; compiled by
Virginia J. Ruehlmann ; illustrations by Samuel J. Butcher.
       p.   cm.
    ISBN 0-8007-1691-4
    1. Christian poetry, American. I. Ruehlmann, Virginia J. II. Butcher, Samuel J.
(Samuel John), 1939–   . III. Title.
PS3568.I28P74   1993
811'.54—dc20   93-6575

Printed in the United States of America

Contents

Cheerful thoughts like sunbeams   8

Take a cup of kindness   12

The sleeping earth awakens   16

Miracles are marvels   21

The unexpected kindness   26

We wouldn't enjoy the sunshine   31

Remember that ideals   33

As we start a new day   36

You are young   43

A baby is a gift of life   48

Love is like magic   50

It does not take a new year   57

A mother's love   58

Fathers are wonderful people   62

Cheerful thoughts like sunbeams
lighten up the darkest fears.
For when the heart is happy
there's just no time for tears.

And when the face is smiling
its impossible to frown.

And when you are high-spirited
you cannot feel low-down.
For the nature of our attitude
toward circumstantial things
determines our acceptance
of the problems that life brings.
And since fear and dread and worry
cannot help in any way,
it's much healthier and happier
to be cheerful every day.

And if you'll only try it
you will find, without a doubt,
a cheerful attitude's something
no one should be without.
For when the heart is cheerful
it cannot be filled with fear.
And without fear the way ahead
seems more distinct and clear.
And we realize there's nothing
we need ever face alone
for our heavenly Father loves us
and our problems are His own.

Take a cup of kindness
mix it well with love.
Add a lot of patience
and faith in God above.

Sprinkle very generously
with joy
and thanks
and cheer.
And you'll have lots of
angel food
to feast on all the year.

The sleeping earth awakens,
the bluebirds start to sing,
the flowers open wide their eyes
to tell us it is spring.

16

The bleakness of the winter
is melted by the sun.
The tree that looked so stark and dead
becomes a living one.

These miracles of Easter
wrought with divine perfection
are the blessed reassurance
of our Savior's resurrection.

19

*M*iracles are marvels
that defy all explanation.
And Christmas is a miracle
and not just a celebration.

For when the true significance
of this so-called Christmas story
penetrates the minds of men
and transforms them with its glory,
then only can rebellious man
so hate-torn with dissension
behold his adversaries
with a broader new dimension.

21

For we can only live in peace
when we learn to love each other
and accept all human beings
with the compassion of a brother.

And it takes the Christ of Christmas.
to change our point of view.
For only through the Christ Child
can we be born anew.

And that is why God sent His Son
as a Christmas gift of love.
So that wickedness and hatred
which the world had so much of
could find another outlet
by following in Christ's way
and discovering a new power
that violence can't outweigh.

And in the Christmas story
of the Holy Christ Child's birth
is the answer to a better world
and good will and peace on earth.

The unexpected kindness
from an unexpected place,
a hand outstretched in friendship,
a smile on someone's face.

A word of understanding
spoken in an hour of trial
are "unexpected miracles"
that make life more worthwhile.

We know not how it happened
that in an hour of need
somebody out of nowhere
proved to be a friend indeed.
For God has many messengers
we fail to recognize
but He sends them when we need them
for His ways are wondrous wise!

So keep looking for an "angel"
and keep listening to hear.
For on life's busy, crowded streets
you will find God's presence near.

We wouldn't enjoy the sunshine
if we never had the rain.
We wouldn't appreciate good health
if we never had a pain.
If we never shed a teardrop
and always wore a smile,
we'd all get tired of laughing
after we had grinned awhile.
Everything is by comparison
both the bitter and the sweet.
And it takes a bit of both of them
to make our lives complete.

Remember that ideals
are like stars up in the sky.
You can never really reach them,
hanging in the heavens high.

But like the mighty mariner
who sailed the storm-tossed sea,
and used the stars to chart his course
with skill and certainty,
you, too, can chart your course in life
with high ideals and love.

For high ideals are like the stars
that light the sky above.
You cannot ever reach them,
but lift your heart up high
and your life will be as shining
as the stars up in the sky.

As we start a new day
untouched and unmarred
unblemished and flawless,
unscratched and unscarred,
may we try to do better
and accomplish much more
and be kinder and wiser
than in the day gone before.

Let us wipe our slates clean
and start over again,
for God gives this privilege
to all sincere men
who will humbly admit
they have failed many ways,
but are willing to try
and improve these new days.
By asking God's help
in all that they do
and counting on Him
to refresh and renew
their courage and faith
when things go wrong
and the way seems dark
and the road rough and long.

What will you do
with this day that's so new?

The choice is yours.
God
leaves
that
to
you.

$\mathcal{Y}$ou are young
and life is beginning
in a wonderful way for you.
The future reaches its welcoming hand
with new, challenging things to do.

And here is a prayer for you
that you'll walk with God every day,
remembering always in whatever you do
there is only one true, righteous way.

May you trust His almighty wisdom
and enjoy the fruit of His love.
And life on earth will be happy
as you walk with the Father above.

$\mathcal{A}$ baby
is a gift of life
born of the
wonder of love.
A little bit of eternity
sent from the Father above.

Giving a new dimension
to the love
between husband and wife.
And putting an
added new meaning
to the
wonder
and
mystery
of life.

*L*ove is like magic
and it always will be.
For love still remains
life's sweet mystery.

Love is unselfish,
understanding, and kind,
for it sees with its heart
and not with its mind!

Love works in ways
that are wondrous and strange.
And there's nothing in life
that love cannot change!

Love gives and forgives.
There is nothing too much
for love to heal
with its magic touch!

Love is the language
that every heart speaks.
For love is the one thing
that every heart seeks!

It does not take a new year
to make a brand-new start.
It only takes the deep desire
to try with all your heart
to live a little better
and to always be forgiving
and to add a little sunshine
to the world
in which
we're living.

A mother's love
is something
that no one can explain.
It is made
of deep devotion
and of sacrifice and pain.
It is endless and unselfish
and enduring come what may
for nothing can destroy it,
or take that love away.

It is patient
and forgiving
when all others
are forsaking,
and it never
fails or falters
even though
the heart is breaking.

It believes
beyond believing
when the world around condemns.
And it glows with all the beauty
of the rarest, brightest gems.

It is
far beyond defining.
It defies all explanation.
And it still remains a secret
like the mysteries of creation—
a many-splendored miracle.

Fathers are
wonderful people,
too little understood.
And we do not sing their praises
as often as we should.

But fathers are
just wonderful
in a million different ways.
And they merit loving compliments
and accolades of praise.
For the only reason Dad aspires
to fortune and success
is to make the family proud of him
and to bring them happiness.
And like our heavenly Father
he's a guardian and a guide,
someone that we can count on
to be always on our side.